Shalome Rides a Royal Elephant

Shalome Rides a Royal Elephant

The Story of the First Jews of Calcutta

Written and illustrated by

Jael Silliman

talking CUB
An Imprint of Speaking Tiger Books

TALKING CUB

125A, Ground Floor, Shahpur Jat,
Near Asiad Village, New Delhi 110049

First published in paperback in Talking Cub by Speaking Tiger Books 2023

ISBN: 978-93-5447-734-8

eISBN: 978-93-5447-736-2

10 9 8 7 6 5 4 3 2 1

Typeset in Crimson Text by Jojy Philip
Printed at:- Pragati Printers, Naraina Inds Area Phase-1

This is a work of fiction. Names, characters, places and incidents either are the product of the author's imagination or are used fictitiously, and any resemblance to actual persons, living or dead, events or locales is entirely coincidental.

For my Vivaan who loves animals

One

It was the year 1792. One morning, in the port city of Surat, I was swinging from branch to branch doing my morning exercises. I gave a really long jump, whoosh, and went flying through the treetops. I climbed to the top of a mango tree and settled down to relax and enjoy the view. I loved sitting way up high watching the silver-grey dolphins dip and fly over the blue-black waters of the Arabian Sea. You see, while I am a champion at so many sports, I can't swim. I watched the dolphins playing and wondered if one day, the dolphins will give me a ride on their backs. They would have to promise not to plunge underwater while I am out at sea with them!

The dolphins swam away. A large ship with many decks and billowing white sails came gliding through the waves. It made

its way to the dock right next to me. I scampered closer to get a better view. I watched ships dock in the busy port to see what kind of people visited my town. I made it my business to know what was going on so I could tell the other monkeys what the humans were up to.

That day I saw a tall man aboard this big ship. He stood out from all the others. He was wearing a maroon and gold turban that was elegantly tied. His robes were long and flowing. Many servants followed him. I knew he must be an important person, and certainly very rich. I heard people call him Shalome. I scratched my head. *Tick tick*—no! I had never heard that name before. I swung down to a lower branch to get a better look at him.

Tick tick tick and a tock. My brain whirred and circled. I, Chanchal, an amazing, brilliant monkey, most respected across many monkey kingdoms, knew I would be a friend and great partner for Shalome. I could teach him a lot about my home, Surat, and about life in this part of the world—after all, everyone needs a *monkeyspective*! And perhaps Shalome could teach me a thing or two. With him, I would live a life of comfort.

My arms and legs sprang from tree to tree as fast as they possibly could to keep up with his horse carriage as it raced to the town. My monkey friends started following me. They, too, wanted to know why I was moving like a flash of lightning through the trees.

Shalome's carriage stopped at the home of a wealthy merchant who, like him, was dressed in robes and a turban. I sat in a banyan tree figuring out my plan of action. *Tick tick and one lick* my brain was spinning as fast as a top in high speed. *Screech!* When it spins at great speed, I know something VERY important will happen—and it sure did!

I heard Shalome and his friends speaking in Arabic. They were in high spirits. They cracked roasted sunflower seeds noisily between their teeth as they sat on carpets in a large garden which had a marble fountain. Shalome told them many stories and he laughed a lot. Music was playing and there was lots of food. A woman danced while balancing a bottle on her head as the musicians played faster and faster. *Whee!* The dance, the music, the sound of the falling water, and the fragrance of flowers put me in an excellent mood. My plan was in place.

Tick, tick, tick. Swoosh! I jumped from the tall tree and landed right in front of Shalome. It was a dramatic entry, even if I say so myself!

I bowed and did a couple of backflips and somersaults. Then after three cartwheels I landed on my tippy toes. The party was clearly impressed. I picked up some branches and danced the Dandiya Raas. It is the most wondrous dance of my country, and I dance it perfectly. I had learned all the complicated steps from a *monkguru* of dance who lived in Baroda. Here was my chance to display my talents. My sticks clicked in perfect rhythm.

Shalome had never seen anything like me before. He was clearly very impressed and clapped loudly. The others joined in and shouted 'Shabash!' 'Mah'ShAllah!' I knew everyone was *monkily* impressed. They clapped even louder than they had for the lady who danced balancing the bottle on her head. *Tick, tick, tick.* I seized the moment. I made my way in dainty steps to Shalome. I curled my long, beautiful, golden furry tail around his arm like a bracelet. Then I looked up at him with my adoring, big, liquid eyes. His dark brown eyes looked back at me admiringly. Then he stroked my beautiful golden fur and said to his friends, 'This is a very clever dancing monkey. I am sure she knows many

more dances and tricks! And, she is lovely, too.' I took a deep curtsy, and my head bobbed from side to side in agreement. I laid my dancing sticks at his feet.

'My name is Shalome Aaron Obadiah ha Cohen,' he told me. From that moment on, just as I had planned, we became friends. I was sure that our *monkership* would last till the very end.

Two

Shalome had made a long journey by ship from an ancient city called Aleppo in Syria. It took him many days to cross the Indian Ocean. A few days after landing he bought a house and started his business in Surat. As he was a very rich man, his friends encouraged him to marry.

One day, a young boy with a huge turban visited Shalome with his parents and elder brother. My head spun round and round, and my eyes popped many times when I found that the young man was actually a very beautiful girl! How could I have guessed that tightly wound in the turban was long, gleaming hair that cascaded down her back in swirling dark curls? Shalome laughed heartily explaining that Najima was so lovely that her parents thought it best to dress her up as a boy when she went out. They did not want everyone to know how beautiful she was. What a funny lot these humans are! What strange things they do, I thought to myself.

Before I could blink an eye, Shalome married Najima. I was quite pleased as Najima was fascinated by me and paid me great attention. When she made trays of sweets, she would always keep many aside for me. My favourite was baklava. The pistachio nuts with honey sauce can take any monkey to heaven—it is so *monkleylicious.*

Soon baby Lunah was born. Najima always consulted me about household matters: 'How should I do this? What is the name of this fruit? What is the best way to cook this vegetable?'

Shalome, 'the Jewish Chief Merchant', was very busy with his work. Of course, I made sure I was there to be of help to Shalome, too, so he could be very successful.

Shalome traded in many precious commodities. I would check the shipments of gold leaf, copper, coral, elephant tusks, indigo, dates, and coffee. Shalome poured out a little of his coffee for me to taste. I spat it out! *Yuck!* Humans! No accounting for what they like. Even though I did not like the taste, Shalome

enjoyed drinking the thick, dark brown liquid. He even offered it in small glasses to his friends who seemed to like it too.

Shalome's shipments came from China, Siam, Zanzibar and Arabia, as well as from across India. Oh! I dreamed of travelling across the seas and meeting monkeys in those distant lands. Would they be very different from me? We monkeys could start trading too! I have a knack for business and am excellent with numbers, just like Shalome. My *monkpals* tell me I have an elephant's memory. My ears may not be anywhere near as large as those of elephants, but they pick up all the important information just as well.

In 1795, Shalome made a trip to Basra. It is a city in a faraway country called Iraq. Shalome assured me that he would return soon and I promised to take good care of Najima and baby Lunah. When he returned, he patted me and thanked me for looking after his home and business.

Shalome decided to leave Surat to set up his business in Calcutta, the capital city. It was all the way on the other side of my exceptionally large country. Shalome was sure we would prosper there, the way we had in Surat. I was ready for the new adventure and agreed to go along with him.

Three

I was keen to see India and travelled with Shalome by carriage and boat down the mighty Ganges River, all the way to Calcutta and to many other cities along the way. Shalome always had so many questions: 'What language are they speaking?' 'What tree is that?' *Tik tick tick,* I always shared my vast store of knowledge with him. He loved chatting with me and would always pet me fondly.

We passed through so many villages where I saw trees, animals, and people I had never seen or ever heard of before. I gathered information from the *monkfriends* along the way so that I could be well informed. I love learning about the world.

Every day, Shalome would sit down to write his diary. In it, he would write about the places we visited, the people he met,

and his business dealings. At these times, I curled my tail around his neck like a necklace to encourage him. When he needed help with local words and customs, I would tell him about those. He was always grateful to me and praised me for my quick wit and sharp intellect.

Shalome wrote in Arabic using the Hebrew script. He always started with the date of his entry. He taught me the importance of Time and why it was important to note each day with a date. I learned that dates are not only important for history but for *monkistory* too.

I wish I could read and write like Shalome. I had hoped he would teach me all he knew about astronomy and the Jewish religion and philosophy. He never did! Humans always underestimate other creatures and how much we know and can learn! I *will* learn to read and write. I will not be satisfied with writing a diary like his *The Sefer Nowrooz.* My diary will be famous across the *monkworld.* Smart humans will read it, too.

Four

Shalome and I arrived in Calcutta in 1798. We took a ghora-gharry to see the main sights of the grand city. *Clop clop clop* we travelled down the main thoroughfare called Chowringhee, Esplanade and visited Government House, Tank Square and Fort William.

I gulped down the water in the large Tank that held drinking water for the town. It was a good place to meet my monkey friends for a drink. The Fort had a moat that could be flooded with water from the river. I liked jumping on the cannons there but never saw a cannonball fly. Shalome said he hoped we never would. He said it is important that we all live in peace.

Calcutta was such an important place. People from across India and the world came to Calcutta to trade and become rich. They spoke so many languages—Portuguese, Chinese, Armenian,

Dutch, English, Greek, Arabic, Persian, and of course, many languages from all over India. All these people lived peacefully together, learning from one another, and enjoying each other's company. Shalome, who was very wise, told me that when people from different cultures and traditions respect and accept each other, all of them grow and prosper.

I made many monkey friends and went to some interesting monkey parties, picnics, and conferences where we had a great deal of *monkfun* together. We especially liked to meet early in the mornings, in the thick jungles that were all around the city. I would wake up at sunrise to hang with my *junglee* relations there. They told me magnificent Jungle Tales. I loved to hear their stories about the great Bengal tigers. These huge tigers were powerful swimmers and ruled the land.

Five

Shalome was the first Jew to set up his home and business in Calcutta. He rented a large house from an Armenian and we lived there alone for a while. I clapped loudly and danced when Najima and the girls arrived a few months later. They were so happy to be with me again too. I took them around to show them the city. Najima was impressed by the stately buildings and the well laid streets. I helped them settle in and all the knowledge I had gathered helped the family with their new life.

Shalome hired Jews from Aleppo and Cochin to work in his businesses. Cochin is way at the tip of India and there were Jews living there for more than a thousand years.

Shalome opened a prayer hall in his home because he was a very religious man. He prayed several times a day after putting a small cap on his head, and every morning he strapped a small leather box to his head which had Hebrew words inside. He knew how to say all the Jewish prayers and which portions of the *Torah*, the sacred book, had to be read each day. He wrote about the prayers in his diary.

His family grew to be very large! God bless him! He had nine children—six girls and three boys. Each of them was jealous of the attention Shalome lavished on me! But I was the one who helped him make his fame and fortune. Naturally, I would be his favourite.

Just as his family grew quickly, so did his businesses and his wealth. He traded in silks, cloth from Dacca, indigo, and precious jewels.

I liked the silks and the jewels most. What beautiful and sparkling colours they had! They were so soft to feel and wrap around me. I visited many princes and merchants who were interested in buying Shalome's beautiful gems and materials. When we went to meet them, Shalome made sure I was dressed in brightly coloured ghagra-choli outfits. These outfits were

made specially for me by a *darzee.* Of all my clothes I liked the emerald and gold outfit the best. Wearing it made me look just *monkificent*! I lived a life of luxury and everyone respected me.

Six

As the community grew, Shalome scouted around for a place where his family and other members of the community could be buried. He discussed the matter with a friend of his. In 1812, his friend presented Shalome with a large plot of land. Most of it was jungle. When Shalome said he would like to pay for it, the friend refused. Shalome did not want to accept such a large gift without giving his friend something grand in return. Right there, without even consulting me, Shalome took a gold and ruby ring—my favourite ring—off his finger and presented it to the nobleman! I was not going to let this happen and before there was even any *tick tick lick,* I jumped up and grabbed the ring from him and clutched it tightly.

Shalome scolded me. He forced the ring out of my grasp and again presented it to the nobleman, and rudely shoved me away. When we returned home, I complained bitterly. 'How could you do that? You know how much I loved to see that large red ruby glow on your finger. I had always wanted to wear it!' Shalome said, 'I am sorry I had never let you try it on. I know you asked me if you could do so many, many times!'

I threw a *monkfit*! I stamped my feet, I wailed, and my tail spun round and round in many circles *whirr whirr whirr*. Shalome, always wise, waited patiently for my tantrum to end. Then he said to me firmly: 'Chanchal, one must never take without giving. And it is always better to give than to receive.'

Seven

Shalome was always looking for new opportunities and new places to explore. I am an explorer too and led many of these expeditions. In 1813, we moved to Chinsurah, on the banks of the Hooghly River. We lived in a grand mansion on the riverbank. I swung from the tall pillars of the verandah and often met my *monkfriends* on the steps leading down to the river. My *monkfriends* told me that Chinsurah was a settlement made by the people from Holland. They spoke Dutch which sounded like double Dutch to me. They, too, had come to Bengal as traders, a long time ago, much before the British.

They built Fort Gustavus. The Fort had a church and a church tower. We would sprint up to the tower and watch the boats go by, just like I used to do in Surat. But I missed the hustle and bustle of Calcutta and the old house which, because I insisted, Shalome kept so other Jews could use it as a prayer hall.

Many friends from Calcutta visited us at Chinsurah. They all came for the weddings of Shalome and Najima's daughters Sarah and Rebecca that were held in our stately mansion. The festivities started with the *mileek,* which is an engagement. Best of all were the sweets and candies. The families of the grooms came with trays laden with flowers and so many sweetmeats, and tons of my favourite baklava. I managed to commandeer several trays to share with my *monkfriends* who had never tasted Middle Eastern sweetmeats before. The loaded trays kept coming and continued even a few days after the weddings.

I was known across Chinsurah as Chanchal, the Queen of the Sweetest Treats. The dinners went on for many days as did the prayers and rituals. I am glad we celebrated several more family weddings in Chinsurah. My *monkfriends* were sure glad too!

Shalome and I visited Calcutta frequently. One important visit took place on a chilly December evening in 1814. Shalome, who was such a handsome man, looked even more noble that day. He wore an elegant purple robe with a big jewel brooch. Najima tied a turban for him that was purple and gold in colour. I told him he looked wonderful and he nodded in thanks. He was attending the celebrations at the home of the British Viceroy. Though I begged to accompany him, he told me this was just not possible, but he would tell me all about it later.

The party was being thrown by the Viceroy to celebrate the signing of a treaty between Britain and many other European countries after a great French Emperor, Napoleon, lost the Battle of Waterloo. *Tick tick tick and lick,* but as much as I thought about it, I could not figure out why a battle fought so far away from Calcutta was a cause for such pomp and fanfare here! Humans! But I am so glad Shalome was there, even though it made no sense at all. I love splendid parties and wished I had been there. I eagerly awaited his return so I could hear all about it from him.

Shalome described a glittering occasion. *Tick tick tick,* I decided one day to visit the sprawling gardens and the grand steps

leading to the majestic mansion. Shalome said it had over sixty rooms without even counting the public halls and verandahs, the banquet rooms, and halls. The party held in the throne room was very luxurious. A long velvet and gold canopy hung atop the throne!

When I asked about the food, Shalome told me he could not eat anything as the food was not *kosher.* I knew all about what kosher is! Jewish people have strict rules about how food is to be prepared and what can and cannot be eaten. However, Shalome had a marvelous evening and met many interesting people from Calcutta's different communities.

Eight

I was so proud when I got to accompany Shalome on his many travels around India for his gem business. One of the most splendid memories is of the over two years we spent in Lucknow. Shalome had been called there by the Nawab. (The Nawab is like a king.)

Even our journey there was exceptional. We set out for Lucknow by boat in 1816. It took us two and a half months to reach Benares, a sacred city for Hindus and especially for me and my tribe. Benares is the home of the Durga Temple, which is also known as the Monkey Temple. The temple is red and yellow to match the colours of the goddess of strength and power. We monkeys give the temple its special character. It is here that we feel truly welcome. We climb and leap everywhere and the

devotees offer us bananas and peanuts. I did not eat any. I was used to much grander food than that! I made many friends there and though I told Shalome about this special place, he never accompanied me when I went visiting.

When we reached Lucknow, Shalome met Nawab Ghazi-ud-din Haidar, who placed a robe of honour on him and Shalome was appointed a court jeweller. Lucknow was a stately city with many splendid buildings and palaces that had domes and minarets. There were many mosques. *Dhum, dhum, dhum,* my heart was pounding with pride. I took my place among the kings of the land. My heart almost stopped beating when Shalome was honoured with a special title of Vazir, meaning advisor to the king. 'Shalome should hold a ceremony and give me that title. After all, I have been his advisor for years!' I told my friends.

When we were in Lucknow, we lived in a very large palace, even grander than our mansion in Chinsurah. It was opposite the house of the British Resident. Our garden had fountains and many large fruit trees. I could climb a different tree every day, and it was much like going to a different café each day! The Nawab told Shalome that we could stay at this splendid place for as long as we liked.

At Lucknow, Shalome rode an elephant alongside the king, which was a special honour. I was disappointed when Shalome said I could not ride along with him. The first day this happened, I wailed and could not be comforted. Then *tick tick lick* my brain started working so fast it whizzed! *Whiz a doodle doo*! I would meet the royal elephants and find out for myself why I was not allowed to ride in the procession. I would speak with this magnificent grey creature that had such big ears—that were almost as big as me! The ears had flowered designs on them made with coloured chalk powder. And the creature had the longest nose I had ever seen! It stretched from its forehead to almost sweep the ground.

I found my way to the elephant stables. Wrapping my tail around the largest elephant's trunk, I captured his heart. He explained there were many rules about who could and who could not ride a royal elephant. He did not like the heavy seat that was placed on his back where many people were seated. It chafed and hurt. He told me blood-curdling tales of how, in battle, he was pierced and fired at by enemy armies. My brain raced: *tick tick tick tick tick lick*! He showed me where arrows and even a bullet had made a hole in his tough, dry, wrinkled skin. To make him feel

better I did a few of my monkey twirls and the other elephants watched too, enchanted by my exceptional dance steps.

Before leaving the stables, the Mother Elephant called me and picked me up with her trunk. She placed me on her back and took me on a ride around the stable. She introduced me to the other elephants and invited me to come back and visit whenever I wished. I asked if I could sit on her forehead and slide down her trunk and she said yes! She stood up, so I was high off the ground and I slid a long way on a thrilling ride to land with a big *thud, dud, dud* in the straw on the floor.

What a thrilling experience it was to visit, entertain, and be entertained at the stables! I will never forget it and I hope they will not either. I do not think they will, as we all know that elephants have long memories. I wonder if their memories are as long as their trunks.

I was sad to leave Lucknow but we left with a bang! I have never been part of such a large retinue. My *monkfriends* were *monkily* impressed. Thirty of the Nawab's soldiers came with us all the way to Calcutta. There were twenty-five young men, seven palanquins, sixty servants, twenty-three sweepers and ten personal servants. I was only disappointed that the Nawab did not send one of the royal elephants back with us!

We returned to Lucknow twice after this, but it was our first stay there and our departure that were so *monkemorable.* Shalome let his son-in-law, Moses Dwek, run his businesses from Calcutta. Many say that while Shalome was the first settler, it was Moses who was the builder of the community. Though Moses also travelled a great deal, I never travelled with him. Shalome always wanted me to himself, and I remained a loyal partner to him.

Nine

Our next exciting adventure was in Punjab which is all the way up north of my huge country. The year was 1822. Shalome went on a special mission invited by a famous king. His name was Maharaja Ranjit Singh, and he was also called the Lion of the Punjab. Shalome told me he was not a lion king, but a human king. He was called the Lion King because he was so strong and brave. These humans! They do come up with strange and misleading titles.

This Person King was the first Maharaja of the Sikh Empire. He had a huge diamond, the most humongous diamond in the world. It is called the Kohinoor. 'Kohinoor' means the Mountain of Light. Ranjit Singh captured it from Shah Shuja of Afghanistan.

I had seen many diamonds before and other precious stones that Shalome would buy and sell. But this time, I, Chanchal, was truly excited. I would get to see the biggest diamond in the world! I dreamed about holding it in my hand. I longed to see how the shape of this grand cut stone would make fantastic patterns as light passed through it. What a vision it would be!

We arrived in the Maharaja's splendid palace. After a few days we went to meet the king. He invited Shalome to the treasury to see the Kohinoor. I was told I could not go along with him. *Tick tick tick and a giant lick.* My brain started whirring fast. I had to plan quickly.

I jumped and hid in one of the many baskets laden with gifts carried by Shalome's men to honour the king. I placed myself in a basket piled with silks so I could peep out and see the Kohinoor. Though I was a little further from it than I would have liked, I did see that it was dazzling and flashing with lights of every colour and was truly very, very large.

Many years later, the Kohinoor was surrendered to Victoria, the Queen of England, the Ruler of the British Empire. I promised, just as the army of monkeys made a bridge to travel to Lanka to get Sita back, I would do just that! I, Chanchal, would lead the monkey army to England to snatch the Kohinoor from the crown and take it back to the Punjab where I had seen it!

Ten

By the time we returned from Punjab, I was sad to see that Shalome was ageing. He was not as strong as he used to be. He was sixty-five years old now. He had trouble with his right eye and had to see doctors about his chest and many other illnesses. He was still a leader of the community. He took me along with him to Calcutta in 1828 to be presented to Lord William Cavendish Bentinck, the first Governor General of India. The British certainly knew how to hold grand parties! But I was not impressed by the food they served. Indian and Jewish food and sweets were much more to my taste!

Shalome now was less interested in his business matters and wanted to put all his troubles behind him. And troubles he did

have. I always listened to his woes to make him feel better. I assured him that the Jewish community and his businesses were in safe hands of Moses Dwek, his son-in-law. When I said that, Shalome nodded and smiled. He said he now liked to spend his time writing and praying.

I have always admired his writing and I have included one of his last poems here. I think my monkey readers as well as other humans can learn a lot from it. It would help to make humans less greedy and could make us monkeys focus a little more on sharing with other creatures. Shalome wrote:

Now turn to me and listen (to) what I say.
Make haste, repent, give alms this very day.
Do not delay and leave it till tomorrow.
The day is short—and the time you cannot borrow.

At the end of his life, he often told me that it is the good deeds you do, and the money you give to those in need, which are most important. On a cold day in February 1836, Shalome closed his eyes forever. How I cried and wailed along with the mourners at his funeral. My heart never quite mended.

Eleven

Now I am old and wise. My brain tick ticks slowly and though it hardly ever whirrs, it ticks better. My eyes don't see as well as they used to, but I notice everything that goes on around me and even see things I missed before. I know what is and what is not important. My golden fur is thinning, and in some places has turned white and has fallen out. I wear my dentures when friends visit. I am not as vain as I used to be. I would say I am now as wise and good as Shalome, who I still miss every day! I am glad he lies in the cemetery, on that large ground with so many trees. I visit often and place a stone on his grave to add to the many other stones that are placed there so all will know that he is revered and remembered.

I read the lines on his gravestone with pride: 'The nobleman, the peer, the honourable, respected and humble Shalome Aaron Obadiah ha Cohen.' I make sure my monkey friends keep an eye on him as he rests there.

Oh! How I loved wrapping my tail around Shalome's arms, ankles, or neck, and he would stroke and pat my back so lovingly, feed me a banana or sometimes give me a delicious piece of baklava, a date-baba, or even a cheese samboosa. I still look forward to the man with his tin trunk coming around to each Jewish home to sell all these Jewish delicacies. I get first pick of whatever I wish to eat, but I have lost my appetite and eat much less.

I celebrate the Sabbath—the Jewish day of rest—with the family. It starts every Friday evening at sunset. Najima, who

אֲדֹנָי
שבת

is very old now, still wears her long, beautifully embroidered *gowan* and lights the oil lamps in the *tirya* and says her prayers. I miss Shalome, who would be formally dressed and take his place at the head of the table. I can still hear his voice singing in praise of the Lord, 'The King of Kings, the Holy One, the Blessed One,' as he raised the goblet of wine and blessed and broke the challah bread. The Sabbath table is still full of family and friends, enjoying the dinner of many courses, singing and chatting through the evening.

On Saturdays the men go say their prayers and return from the prayer hall to sit down to a gigantic meal just as Shalome used to do. I enjoy the smells of the hamim, the delicious Sabbath lunch, which cooks all night! I enjoy tasting the chicken stuffed with rice and condiments.

The family treats me with great respect as they do other elders of the community. I am always invited to the Sabbath meal but I miss going with Shalome to look up at the vast sky to count seven stars to mark the end of the Sabbath. When he could no longer see so well it was I who would tell him that Sabbath is over.

I think of all the wonderful wedding celebrations when Shalome's children got married. Those days he so enjoyed seeing and eating from all the trays of candies and molasses sent for the *toowaffah* ceremonies, on Saturday nights before each wedding.

I, Chanchal, am too old to climb a tree. I, who was so swift of foot and fleet of hand, sit on an easy chair on the verandah and look out at the busy bazaar. My brain *tick tick tick ticking,* slowly but very surely. I am now busy completing my diary and writing the final chapter.

If not for my diary, the human and animal world would know so little about the adventures, trials, and triumphs that Shalome and I had together. From my tale all will learn about Shalome and how he had travelled from Syria and Iraq to India. They will know that we two, through our long and fabulous partnership, had met kings, nawabs, and Viceroys. They will marvel at the

Chanchal chronicles
OLD MONK

numerous honours showered upon us. I still find it so unfair that I was not given the Robe of Honour nor was I allowed to ride the royal elephant. Humans always take all the credit!

Together Shalome and I made great fortunes and because of us other Jews came to settle in Calcutta. We lived in palaces and in British and Dutch settlements. We were revered by all. Honouring Shalome's dying wishes, we left money for various charities.

In monkey kingdoms I will be well-known for my scholarship. This diary will be widely read and passed down through the generations. Other monkeys already vie to be as learned as I. Just as we monkeys all know of the sage Rafiki who lived in Africa, famed for his profound powers of meditation, I, Chanchal, am known as one of the greatest historians.

Other Jewish traders from across the Middle East followed Shalome and are building synagogues, schools and hospitals, and setting up important businesses in Calcutta. The city is also growing bigger and more roads and imposing buildings are being built. People call it 'the city of palaces'. To the horror of many of my *monkfriends*, the jungle is being cleared and many of us are becoming homeless. They tell me that some important streets are being lit by gaslight and there are plans afoot to build a gigantic market called Sir Stuart Hogg Market. It will sell everything there is in the world. When it opens, *In Sh'Allah* I will do some shopping there.

Jewish traders are going across the sea from Calcutta to places even further away! Jewish merchants have started businesses in Rangoon, Singapore, Djakarta, Hong Kong, and even Shanghai! I know a lot about these places now by reading the Jewish newspaper the *Paerah*. But I have not visited them, and neither did Shalome. We were happy exploring so many parts of India.

I was so clever to have taken a chance on Shalome the very day he arrived in Surat. I am glad that I wrapped my tail around his arm and stood devotedly by his side throughout his long life. I encouraged and helped him in his business, travels, and learning.

I, Chanchal, played an important part in this splendid tale of the Jews of Calcutta. That part in my diary (for those of you who are interested in learning more) is called 'Monkey Business in Calcutta'!

Author's Note

The story is based on the diary of my great, great, great, great, great grandfather, Shalome Obadiah ha Cohen, the first Jewish settler in Calcutta. All the facts and stories are historically substantiated.

I thank my sister, Lahava, and my brother, Albert, my friends Anuradha Chatterji and Anindyo Roy, and Meredith Bond for discussing the writing of this story with me.

Jael Silliman is the author of several books, scholarly papers and popular articles for newspapers and magazines on gender, development, race, social justice, women's rights issues, and writes about her community—the Baghdadi Jews of Calcutta. Her books relating to Kolkata's cultural history include *Jewish Portraits, Indian Frames: Women's Narratives from a Diaspora of Hope*, two novels, *The Man with Many Hats* and *The Teak Almirah.* Her most recent co-authored publications are *Where Gods Reside: Kolkata's Scared Places* and *Adda! The College Street Coffee House, and India in Celebration.* She has created a digital archive on the Calcutta Jewish community at https://indianjewishcenter.co.il/baghdadi-jews/

Read more in Talking Cub

talking
CUB

Mishti the Mirzapuri Labrador

Gillian Wright

Illustrated by Anitha Balachandran

'Mishti had worked out for herself how to get people out of bed in the morning. You could be lying happily asleep and Mishti would hop up beside you, and lie with her full weight across your stomach. If that failed, she would climb on your chest and lick your face.'

Mishti, a little golden Labrador born in Mirzapur on the banks of the Ganga, is adopted by two people from Delhi, called Gilly and Mark. It is the beginning of many adventures they will have, indoors and outdoors, as they learn to live together and become a family.

Full of love, mischief and great charm, told in gloriously readable prose and complemented with delightful illustrations, this is a book for dog-lovers and story-lovers of all ages.

When I Grow Up I Want to be a Tiger

Prerna Singh Bindra

Illustrated by Maya Ramaswamy

'This is a must-read book for children interested in wild tigers. Prerna Bindra highlights the remarkable relationship between the mother and cubs in the most engaging of ways.'—Valmik Thapar

Tigers don't talk (well, at least not in 'people' language). Tigers don't have names either. But then T-Cub is a very special tiger cub and he wants to tell you his story. It's about his life in a forest in India and his animal friends (and foes) including monkeys, peacocks and elephants.

T-Cub is naughty, curious, lovable and brave (and sometimes scared too!). He is living the good life of a wild tiger—prowling the forest, loved by his Ma, teased by his sister. He is learning the ways of the jungle, to hunt, to be a tiger... And then one day his mother vanishes and T-Cub learns another lesson—it isn't easy being a tiger.

The Tiger of the River

Adrian Pinder

Illustrated by Maya Ramaswamy

The incredible story of the tiger of the river, Matisha—the majestic mahseer fish

Somewhere in the Kaveri River where the water rushes through a deep gorge, lives a very special fish called Matisha, one of the largest and most beautiful freshwater fish on Planet Earth.

Matisha delights in exploring her mysterious underwater world and meets a vast array of magnificent animals with whom she shares the river and the surrounding jungle. She is fascinated by the many strange fish of all shapes and sizes and the large powerful animals like tigers and elephants which occasionally visit the river. She dodges the attentions of hungry birds, crocodiles and otters who would love to gulp her down as prey. She also learns about humans, who are sometimes far more dangerous than the animals around her.

In this dream-like story, follow the wonderful adventures of Matisha as she migrates upstream to lay her precious eggs. Illustrated beautifully by Maya Ramaswamy with vibrant colours, the invisible world that lives below the waters of the river and in the Western Ghats come alive through the eyes of a fascinatingly beautiful, yet critically endangered species.